These are stunning poems of "Godhunger," and doubt, flood and drought, praise and rage—no easy devotional exercises as the poet climbs "bloodykneed toward the Lord," both bereft and filled with grace. Emma Galloway Stephens writes about holiness that is taxing and magnificent.
— **Jill Peláez Baumgaertner,** poetry editor, *The Christian Century*

In *No Billboard Gospel*, Emma Galloway Stephens sees the unseeable—a poet's charge—alive with ache and trembling. She beckons us forward with a power kin to her grandmother's buckwheat-and-butter spells, biscuits rising like small miracles. With these feral hard-won truths she wakes us with wonder and witness.
—**Glenis Redmond,** author of *Over Yonder: A Poet's Exploration of South Carolina State Parks, Part II*

In *No Billboard Gospel*, the poems of Emma Galloway Stephens inhabit a landscape of red clay, summer heat, winding rivers, and lonely highways. They are astonishing visions of a New South remembering its past and beyond, back to the Holy Land, back to the Whirlwind.
—**Steven Peterson,** author of *Walking Trees and Other Poems*

From a place "waist deep where no angel can follow," Emma Galloway Stephens eschews the dumbed-down platitudes of billboard gospel to proclaim the joys of a life lived in faith and rich in family, prayer, and truth. These skillfully crafted poems perch at the nexus of earth and spirit.
—**Richard Allen Taylor,** author, *Letters to Karen Carpenter and Other Poems*

No Billboard Gospel

poems

Emma Galloway Stephens

NO BILLBOARD GOSPEL

Emma Galloway Stephens

Anaheim, CA • solumpress.com

Solum Literary Press
6597 East Camino Vista #3
Anaheim, CA 92807

solumpress.com

PAPERBACK ISBN 978-1-965169-11-7
EBOOK ISBN 978-1-965169-12-4

Cover art and design by Sarah Christolini.
Interior design by Grace Russo.
Author photo by Evan Taylor. Used with permission.

LIBRARY OF CONGRESS CATALOGUING-IN-PUBLICATION DATA
Name: Stephens, Emma Galloway, author.
Title: no billboard gospel / emma galloway stephens.
Description: Anaheim, CA: Solum Literary Press, 2026.
Identifiers: LCCN 2026932150
ISBN 978-1-965169-11-7 (print)
ISBN 978-1-965169-12-4 (Kindle)
Subjects: BISAC: POETRY / Subjects & Themes / Religious / Places / Women Authors
LC record available at https://lccn.loc.gov/2026932150

For Samuel

Table of Contents

NO BILLBOARD GOSPEL

In the Spirit on the Lord's Day

I was in the Spirit on the Lord's day
driving down the lonely highway
covered in cracks—I lost my way
once the two lanes turned to one—
no side to side, only back or through
and nighttime melted out of day.
In the hills you can smell the hunger
of the night creatures—trees grow
features. Kudzu beards and streetlamp
eyes flicker in the dark. In the deadnight
alive with fireflies, a whisper like Eden
hisses in my mind—*The long night comes*
for you, firstborn. Are you ready?

I. Drought

River Song I

Across our milltown's river,
I see mountains ripple

cobalt in spring, copper in autumn,
lovely in every light.

I could wade into the water,
chin deep, to reach the other side,

let the river swallow me, slay me
so I could rise again,

this time a mountain girl,
born of the water and the word,

barefoot in a green eternity,
white-eyed, full of prophecy.

In spirit and truth, I stand on the bank,
barefoot in sand slick as velvet.

This town is not my home—
it's a passing place.

But I'm dirt-deep, ankle bound
in clay, red stains to my knees.

But when this town lets me go—
who knows?

Psalm 4

Psalm 4:4

Answer me, God. I'm drowning in venom
pooled under my tongue. A serpent boils
in my throat, a knot. You vowed
vindication. But my voice is a coil.

These hallowed halls are mold choked.
The moldings crack with water weight.
The carpets squelch with liquid lies
that pour from our exalted heights.

Listen, God—I can't breathe in here.
Take my anger; make it sinless,
wash it white in holy fire,
the kind that vapors vipers into ash.

I cannot give a sacrifice of praise—
will you accept a sacrifice of rage?

Billboard Gospel

CHRIST IS KING
above the Cracker-Barrel All-Day Breakfast ad
together seem to say
that Christ and pancakes both will satisfy.
For other hungers, look no further—

the next exit takes you to
an Adult Superstore
Called BedTyme Stories—
so says the neon above
a plywood plaque that hollers

GOD IS LOVE.
It is appointed unto man once to
die, and after that,

the Outlet Mall

(above an ad declaring Jesus Saves).

You can find gods at the flea market,
the theme park, the Burger King—
the Golgatha string on I-85
lifts high every purchase we hope will save us.
Adjust the price of silver for the inflation and you'll
know

These advertisements
that guarantee salvation
at the affordable price of grace
promise nonspecific savings for unclear services
that I assume cost somebody something.

the birthright
of the believer in America,
the pottage and the goat stew,
delicious ash in the highwaymen's mouths.

Contusion

There's an ache in my heart
like an ache in the jaw—

a raw, swollen contusion
of gums and teeth,

a ragged heat that rolls
from the side of my tongue

to my inner ear,
throwing me off balance,

pulling me sideways,
dragging me down.

I can't eat with ease,
though this ache makes me

hollow, hungry
for food I've never tasted.

This Godhunger
gnaws me empty—

my starvation for truth
in the deadheat disease of drought.

If a snake offered me
a magic apple

saying this will take
the ache away, I'd bite.

I'd let the sugar sting
my porous teeth

I'd let the syrup pool
in my bleeding gums

I'd let the juice run
down my chin, into my chest.

Liturgy I

I spend my Sundays talking to the dead,
kneeling in the haunted house of God.
I light my candles, ring my bell,
burn incense like a bridge.
I whisper words as old as those who wait—
dark watchers on the other side
of darker glass—bold to ask:
        Who fills the chalice in my hands?
        Who lifts the table with the bread?
        Whose voice is this that fills my throat?
        What rapture lies ahead?
I hear the answers Sunday's said before:
Three knocks from someone standing at the door.

Saint Joan the Opossum

St. Joan the Opossum with her one white eye
saw God, who left her half blind
and happier than the richest king.
St. Joan won't lack for anything.

St. Joan eats honeylocust cheerios
and tells every critter she knows
The kingdom of God is a whisker away.
Her neighbors whisper, but Joan, she stays.

Some ask, *how can a possum know*
if God's kingdom comes or goes?
She says *the weak will make the mighty weep*
with all the secrets that they keep.

St. Joan the Opossum keeps her peace,
calling all God's critters to the feast.

The Last Summer of the Kumquat Tree

The tree bore fruit for one summer only.
A cluster of kumquats grew like a tumor in the heart;
the branches couldn't hold more than one year's yield,
each fruit as orange as the last morning
I held my brother's baby boy.

Some gravestones are no taller than weeds
blooming by the railroad tracks—one of them is his.
The wheel turns with brutality and haste.
One summer of hail and hurricane, and he is home,
though home for him is hallowed, ours a waste.

No coffin should be built that small.
No coffin should be built at all.

Poetry of Witness

then I tell them I saw
a parade of dead children
led by the antler man in his baggy suit

he put a little flag
in each cold gray hand
said *smile for the cameras*

no jury can convict a nameless arm
whose fingers are faces
that twitch from hell's sleeve

let me run to the hills
older than hell
let me eat locusts

let kudzu claim me like a tin trailer
let the hills swallow me
milk me into honey

and feed me to the black bears
so my tongue is one with the river
and even I can't understand me anymore

II. Flood

River Song II

I need to swim in God
like a river—
to drown.

I want to be a catfish
feeding on holy muck
at the bottom of the lake

that silvers
God's ankles
around the white throne.

Sixty-six books
and prayer
is not enough.

I want to swing between God's arms,
a child between her parents
flying down the gravel road:

one for the money,
two for the show,
Father, Son,

and Holy Ghost.

Merciless Heat

Summer in its fullness dreams of autumn.
Its emerald optimism is a scrim
that shimmers in the heat. The beat
of wings above the rotting roadkill,
white bones blazing in a sunny hell,
predicts the golden death that is to come.

The red earth hates the wet but rainless boil
that cooks creatures, gardens, crops,
uncoils the creeks. Heat feels like hatred,
relentless, sterile, futile, gulping good,
and greedy in its gaze. In summer, air is water,
crushing lungs in hazes running aimless

on the crooked asphalt strangling the earth.
Always autumn brings rebirth.
Trees drink the heat that dyes their hands red,
bleeds them dead. Redemption falls like death
on trees, and rises like the smoke of burning leaves,
like golden wheat, like dry, cold air.
Like mercy.
Like prayer.

River Wade

I'm too far from home
to know my name—
waiting on the wrong side

of that wide river. My thoughts,
my prayers are leaves in eddies—
nothing's steady. Mother told me

God will hold me. My hands
are empty. His words clot
between my toes, this wet sand.

Woes waver like catfish,
bottom feeding in the in-
between, silt-colored,

sight unseen. Doubt, a long-
legged fly, skirts but can't sink.
God knows I am ice-

boned, unhomed, knee-
deep, half-asleep, seeing,
not believing in the night.

The Devil Beats His Wife

When the devil beats his wife,
rain and sunshine fall together.

Hell's housewife knows her husband's days
are few—the rain falls rain on sun on rain.

The devil's a mobster, a debt collector—
his wife waxes hell's nine floors,

washes its sooty windows.
It's a house of slamming doors.

But slowly she learns not to flinch
when he crashes through the kitchen—

a woman knows when a man
is at the end of his rope.

She knows his oily well is nearly dry—
and so's the sky.

Saint Joan the Opossum and Friar Raven

Fra. Raven came to see St. Joan,
his mind alive with questions on the wind.
The trees succumbed to aphids one by one,
the nests fell solemnly upon the ground,
the fires ate the bracken and the grass,
the streams ran hollow, starved for rain and snow.
Dead beasts are feasts for crows and kin,
but Fra. Raven could not rejoice—*Why*
should I fare well while all my neighbors starve?
The city of the woods was crumbling fast,
and even crows have sorrow for the lost—
for famine eats us all, both bird and beast.

The possum said, *It's well that you should mourn,*
for mourning is the morning of the soul.
That all of us can gain from others' loss
is evidence of grace in spite of sin.
Take this yearning for a greener world,
your pity for your neighbor Deer and Bear,
and let your grief grow generosity.
Leave gifts for those who feed the hungry mouths—
cry warning for the hunter on the trail.

Containment at Table Rock

The mountain ain't done burning yet.
Is this fire an act of God
or of a careless cigarette?
Is the fire that eats the trees
slander or apocalypse?
Behold the rot the fire reveals—
hear what slips the burning bush's lips.
God help both heedless hiker
and widowed possum, babies on her back.
Fire burns both saints and sinners black.

I Go Down to the River to Pray

I go down to the river to pray.
Its water tumbles to the Mississippi,
a major artery, open to the open sea,
alive with salt and electricity.
The ocean is the world's big heart,
sounding its depths, eroding,
overtaking the heights,
every beat a thunderstorm, a hurricane,
a tide. Everything I am, inside.

I think of all holy rivers, life givers,
made of reeds and blood and crocodiles,
carrying boats and baskets for miles,
washing our wounds and healing
disease. They are deaf to our pleas,
all microbe and no matter. Whole cities
thirst, parched for everlasting water.
We crave a river as a river craves the sea.
I crave a current where my prayers can carry me.

Snakebelly Low

I grew up snakebelly low.
            Preacher passed me a viper
when I was ten years old,
            its scales quicksilver
in my tender hands.

Snakebelly low meant closer to God.
            We broke bread over possum stew,
communion over collards. We were
            protesting protestants,
wise as serpents,

dumb as doves. Preacher told us
            who to love. A viper bit my father—
he caught the fever. Mother wound
            his purple hand in gauze,
gaze heavenbent.

I was grown before one bit me.
            Preacher said I'd lost my faith,
backslidden, fallen from the way—
            but I'd found it,
caught red-handed, climbing bloody-knuckled
                        toward the Lord.

No Billboard Gospel

Romans 6:6

Let me smell the good red earth—
blood iron and hookworms under my nails.
I'm waist deep where no angels follow,
digging a grave for the man who martyred me.

Let me sink a shovel into sin
and carve a hole fit for midnight burial.
Moonlight luster burns his two-piece polyester
and the shock of recognition on his purple face.

Let me baptize this old man in groundwater,
six feet under, give the good earth blood to drink.
His old heart is the bread I break.
Let this red clay unmake my worst mistakes.

Let me remember the violent grace
that carves saints out of sinner's chests,
which no broadcast or billboard gospel
could ever resurrect or lay to rest.

III. Spring

River Song III

Mama doesn't know
that at night I swim in the river—

me and the midnight moccasins
slither in the silver water,

bathing in moon wine,
ankle deep in mud like velvet.

Sister salamanders, slick and kind,
pull my worries from my mind.

My hair unwinds. God's ribbons.
The water makes me forget myself.

How lovely, not to know myself,
my own name a blank,

my being an eddy, a pebble,
a water moccasin, a salamander.

I let the water wrap around me
the way prayers wrap around God.

He drinks them all.
The river rises. My body falls.

March on Paris Mountain

I feel beneath my feet the great greening
of the earth. March comes roaring, bares
its teeth, rattles its bones against the rocks.
Those deep down dear things coil tight
and spring—ferns unfurling, trees in flush;
the flesh of earth is warming, though storms
shout hell and high water in the hills.
There is no winter yet unending—

only resurrection and revival waiting,
our pages turned by hands unresting.
The wheel that turns is not done turning.
This greening of the earth is just a dream
of dawning—dark is just the future yawning
before it splits all mountains open at the seams.

Liturgy II

I spend my Sundays talking to the dead,
knowing our conversation is more or less
one-sided, but nonetheless essential,
a raft adrift on the Jordan or the Thames
or the Mississippi River, held aloft by gathered tears
of turtles, martyrs, angels, crocodiles, a testament
to the endurance of the water and the word.
The cord connecting us is part plumbline, part prayer,
a lifeline long as ripples on the river that rolls into waves,
the echoes of a pebble dropped at the fountainhead
two thousand years ago, extending holy hands
to touch my temples, bless my tombs, anoint my head.

Angel Unawares

The woman is unlovely.
She pushes a stroller
full of everything but a baby.
Her language is thick syrup
stuck in the tree of her throat.
She wears a jumble of clothing,
a coat of many colors.
She has money enough for soup
at this underground café—
its mismatched couches laden
with bristling adolescents,
puffer vests and pleats.
She does not see them.
She sits across from a motley friend,
lowering the soup before him,
muttering incantations heard of old
in halls of golden kings,
folding her hands before her
                                        like crooked wings.

Roadkill Sonnet

I found a possum in the road,
her remains unholy, but whole.
In the moonlight, her blood ran gold,
her mouth agape. Hide without soul.

I turned on my hazards, grabbed a towel
from the trunk. My gloved hands, a bowl
for her bowels. Overhead, an owl
mourned. I held her. I took a trowel

and furrowed her a roadside bed.
We were made for Eden—not for pain,
but full bellies and flowerbeds.
In some other dawn we'll meet again

where saints of every shape lay down their loads.
No more death. No more sorrow. No more roads.

The Whirlwind

after Johnny Cash

This morning, I walked in a whirlwind
among the thorn trees. The red deer
were not afraid of me. Crows called
from their cloisters in the rocks. Mist
left holy waters on my skin.

Wind rides the mountain's sides
to the clouds that crown the peak.
The blown pines speak, the laurels
and elders clap their hands,
breezes ripple wiregrass tides.

I've always heard that God is King
of rocks and seas, of skies and trees,
but churches are the house of God—
not the mountainhead or whalebelow.
But Sinai says otherwise, and Jonah, too—

imagine what the willows do when God rests
in garden lees he breathed. Cathedral arches
borrow beauty from the trees. Creation sings
because its father has a voice. And if his voice
is in the whirlwind, it might even be in me.

The Magnolia Years

Joel 2:25

The magnolia bloom begins
as an egg, bright-shelled.
It opens—it smells
of incense at Easter, heavy
as a memory of my mother
with her Sunday pearls.
It unfolds: within, a bulb,
benevolent, blemishless—in time
brown like apple peel,
ripe with decay. Every petal
falls away. The pod within:
a crown of thorns, a dozen eyes
blinking from its bristled hide.
Its seeds are sticky—like blood
nearly dried. They fall below,
every drop a holy deed,
where, given thirty years,
there grows a tree.

Stone Houses

My father loves houses made of stone,
and dreams one day that he can call one home.
He says there's an appeal to the feel of rock.
Instead of vinyl or brick, a locked-
in-ness, a Henge-ness, organic and real.
Because he loves them, so do I—
I point them out when we drive by
one on a trip—my spouse laughs at it,
my observing the obvious, my spit-
and-image-ness. I notice cows and trains,
I stand on porches when it rains
and mutter something like "we needed this."
Fathers can be walls of rocks. I miss
the steady patter of his voice behind the wheel
on our vacations, the constant stone and steel
that formed the pattern of my life.
We see each other now as grownups do. I'm a wife,
building walls of my own. And nothing's wrong—
he's well, I'm well; he's strong, I'm strong.
He built my foundations, laid my cornerstone.
No matter where I am, I'm never far from home.

Sunday Mornings

Mother tells me her grandmother made biscuits
on a countertop from a formless void
of White Lily flour, measuring with her hands
and eyes. A kind of magic,
those spells of buckwheat and butter.
She'd summon biscuits from the flour,
shaping them in her white, warm palms.
My mother doesn't believe in her own magic,
leveling her flour with the flat edge of a knife,
measured and even as her heartbeat and her life.

Mother made biscuits in the freezer aisle.
Every Sunday of my childhood,
she baked a full dozen: uniform, anonymous.
She apologized to the ghost of her grandmother
while rolling the little cold moons in sugar and cinnamon,
laying them in rows for the oven's mouth and mine.
I woke to the ministry of biscuits and orange juice
laid on a technicolor quilt of comic strips.
I bit into the memories my mother made from scratch,
the only homily I know by heart.

This Feral Faith

This feral faith that holds
my head under the water,
that rolls me in the mud,
twigs and leaves—makes me a daughter

of a ragged royalty. I am skinned
knees, ripped jeans, bruised brow.
Incense in my sanctuary—pine straw,
dandelion down. Prayers are wind-

strewn seed. Possum-plod and deer
spring, my creed. Crown me
with daisies so I may cast them down
at the mountain-root, my father's throne.

Restoration

In the will, they left me a house I did not want—
dated, choked with asbestos, mold, and rot.
But I lifted the linoleum laid in '86,
unveiling oak floors glowing in the opal light
pooling from stained glass I found behind warped paneling.
I stripped the drop ceiling and its curdled tiles,
revealing airy vaults with cedar beams, plumb and spry.
I found the house's cornerstone unweathered and uncracked.

All that's crooked in this crooked house is new,
glued in haste, a reaction to the fashion of its time,
fading, festering under the Sun
who nevertheless persists in merciful abundance,
shining through the narrow windows that remain,
letting in the light and locking out the rain.

Acknowledgments

Poems in this book first appeared in the following publications:

Blood Orange Review ("Contusion")
Christian Courier ("I Go Down to the River to Pray")
Clayjar Review ("St. Joan the Opossum")
Door is a Jar Literary Magazine ("River Song I," "River Song III")
Ekstasis Magazine ("Angel Unawares," "Snakebelly Low," "The Magnolia Years")
Heavy Feather Review ("The Devil Beats His Wife")
J Journal ("Poetry of Witness," forthcoming)
Kosmeo Magazine ("Merciless Heat")
Paddler Press ("Liturgy II" as "Liturgy I," "Sunday Mornings")
Persephone Literary Magazine ("This Feral Faith")
The Christian Century ("The Last Summer of the Kumquat Tree")
The MacGuffin ("March on Paris Mountain," "No Billboard Gospel")
The Raven's Muse ("River Wade")
Skipjack Review ("Containment at Table Rock")
The Windhover ("Restoration")
Thimble Literary Magazine ("River Song II")
Wayfarer Magazine ("Roadkill Sonnet")

This book would not exist without the love and support of my community. I include my endless thanks to the following friends and family:

To poets Suzanne Cleary, Denise Duhamel, Rick Mulkey, Kari Gunter-Seymour, and Glenis Redmond, for providing much-needed publishing advice prior to this book's acceptance at Solum Literary Press.

To poet Chelsea Fraser, for being a sounding board for my haphazard ideas and an early reader of most of the poems printed here.

To author Michelle Grover and poets Joshua Blankenship and Mandy Blankenship for providing me a platform for reading my work and welcoming me into the Greenville poetry and publishing community.

To my fellow Sprinters, poet/author Christiana Doucette and author/essayist/editor/podcaster Kendra Winchester. If I had not met with them for an hour-and-a-half writing session once a week for the last two years, these poems would not have been written at all.

To my parents, Jesse and Rhonda Galloway, for their unconditional love and prayerful support, and for instilling in me a love of words, good books, the Good Book, and Christ.

To Samuel, my love, for believing in me and my work, for his thoughtful, helpful critiques of early drafts of these poems, and for helping me keep the faith.

www.ingramcontent.com/pod-product-compliance
Lightning Source LLC
LaVergne TN
LVHW051021080826
845145LV00009B/2740

* 9 7 8 1 9 6 5 1 6 9 1 1 7 *